DAZE OF OUR LIVES

RIO DELORES

authorHOUSE®

AuthorHouse™
1663 Liberty Drive
Bloomington, IN 47403
www.authorhouse.com
Phone: 1 (800) 839-8640

Published by AuthorHouse 09/17/2018

ISBN: 978-1-5462-5925-1 (sc)
ISBN: 978-1-5462-5924-4 (e)

Library of Congress Control Number: 2018910597

Print information available on the last page.

Any people depicted in stock imagery provided by Getty Images are models, and such images are being used for illustrative purposes only. Certain stock imagery © Getty Images.

This book is printed on acid-free paper.

Because of the dynamic nature of the Internet, any web addresses or links contained in this book may have changed since publication and may no longer be valid. The views expressed in this work are solely those of the author and do not necessarily reflect the views of the publisher, and the publisher hereby disclaims any responsibility for them.

I Dedicate this book to

Delores Brown
Cynthia Brown
QuinTina Smith
Jalila Carter
Willie 'ogSmith' Govan
Rest in Spirit

CONTENTS

Introduction ix

Unconsciousness

Innocence 1
Imitation 7
Action/Consequence 14
Perception 19
Belief 24

Pre-Consciousness

Contradiction 31
Curiosity 36
Assimilation 40
Consternation 47
Freewill 51

Consciousness

Cognizance 57
Elimination 65
Modesty 69
Actualization 73
Autonomy 79

Acknowledgements 85
About the Author 87

INTRODUCTION

Compared to when I was younger, now the days go by almost in a blur. I can remember when I use to sit back and say to myself, "Man I'll be glad when this is all over." See in those days I'd spent most of my youth in and out of group homes and institutions.

Those days molded and prepared me for the challenges I invite into my present life. Those days were necessary in order for me to become the man that I am these days. And I will say that I am not necessarily content with who I've become but I am sure proud. Proud in a humble way.

When we become stuck in our own way of thinking or the way we perceive things to be, we paint a picture that only we can interpret. And we eventually become a part of that picture. We pass this picture on to the next generation. Then you realize that we have a nation of misunderstood paintings. A child's future is only as promising as the values that they acquire'.

PART 1

UNCONSCIOUSNESS

INNOCENCE

"Bitch come here! Get in the car."

One of the masked men said to a nearby black woman while grabbing her firmly by the arm.

"But I aint do nothin'." The woman proclaimed. She was clearly as shocked as the rest of us during that hot summer day on the east side of Detroit. I can't really remember what year it was but I do remember it was around the late 80s maybe '87. The emergence of the crack era. A major part of history for the blacks in America. In my opinion, the crack epidemic is just as significant to black history as slavery is. We watched our mothers and fathers turn to their lowest points.

"I said get the fuck in" The man growled.

I can remember being so shocked that I slowly walked backwards into a pole hurting my head. I was around eight or nine years old and seeing the weapons these brothas had jumped out of the car with was frightening. It had happened so fast by the time I realized what was going on they had the lady in the car and was burning rubber around the corner.

A bunch of us kids had just come from one of the churches that served free lunches to the community. I had nearly shitted that lunch right up out of me. That was my first time seeing a real camouflaged machine gun in person. And definitely my first time seeing someone get kidnapped. But it was real in the field. Brothas and sistas were either being turned out by the money being made from selling the rocks or the way the rocks had made them feel.

Even in my young years I realized the affect that this new way of getting high had on black people in the inner cities of America.

For a few days after that incident, I'd wondered what had happened to that lady and if those guys had killed her. I'd eventually seen her back on the block and whatever she may have endured seemed to not have bothered her too much because she was right back to chasing that glass dick.

It took me to gain understanding through experiencing my own vices but I will get into that later on in the book. I'd caught on to how the system worked the older I became.

I could remember being in a children's home and being one of the only kids "academically fit" if you will, to attend the public schools there in a suburban town of Detroit called Redford. I was around thirteen years old at this time but I can recall being sent to this predominately white school and even after being considered smarter than most of the other kids at the home, I still wasn't smart enough to be in general classes. They labeled kids like me emotionally impaired. Which according to the person(s) who'd thought of the word, is the inability to learn due to repeated behavioral and psychological challenges.

Now no matter how smart I may have scored on those competency tests, they still placed my black ass in classes with kids who'd had learning disabilities.

Me being black and from the towns children's home was the reason I'd been given that label and I'll never forget how they tried to convince me that since I was from a broken household that it had effected my learning ability. I was told that it will take time for me to work my way into regular classes. Come to find out, a lot of those kids were actually in those classes due to behavioral problems. It was actually entertaining.

I'm here to tell you, going to those white schools gave me the sense of pride I have for my race and who I am now. I had to stand up to a lot of bullshit in those schools.

Back when Spike Lee produced the movie Malcolm X, I remember going to school one morning wearing a black winter skull cap with X on the front proudly. I looked forward to going to school that day wearing that hat. As I'd expected, one of the school's tough guys had made a statement that I will never forget. He seen me coming down the hall and says, "Take that damn nigger hat off".

"Fuck you mutha fucka!" Was my response. I stared long and hard ready for whatever he wanted to bring. I'd grown up smaller than the average so I've always had that complex issue. No one, especially some white boy was going to make me take off my hat.

Compared to that boy, I was alot smaller but down for the cause. I'd ran into that guy a few more times over a one year time span and we'd eventually gotten an understanding.

A lot was going on during this era of my life. You had the Rodney king verdict, you had Magic Johnson reveal acquiring the HIV virus, the dope game had started turning into the rap game for young brothas around the country.

From 1989 through 1993 I'd gone through some troubles. Those four years were a blur. My whole life an adventure. Being a man now I can say that I'd seek the attention that every other normal kid wanted. But instead of being taught the right values and given the reality of my place in this society, I was given an impression that I was special and that I should look at where I came from as an unfortunate and depressing situation. So I grew up with the frame of mind that I was special and that everyone will understand. My parents failed me and the world owed me something. Yes! This is what they instill into the average child that has gone through the system.

In reality, the average black man ends up in prison,

Pre-mature death, or homosexual. Now I'm sure most of you that read this book have at one time or another heard of those statistics. Why? Because this is what was designed and there was no one there to instill in me what it took for me not to become one of those average black men. I'd slowly started to develop a chip on my shoulder and by the time Id reached a naive fourteen years of age, I'd thought I had my mind made up on what it was I wanted to do.

That was to simply play the streets. Now don't get me wrong I'd always had a drive to be a successful individual, but I had been influenced in the wrong way. I had people that I looked up to just like any other child did.

I'd been in and out of placements and staying with different relatives coming and going as I pleased.

I would run away from certain places they'd send me to. I'd had a foolish way of seeking attention, so foolish that at the end of the day I'd created a paper trail.

I could remember being punched in the face by one of my mother's boyfriends. That experience at six years old I believe contributed to my no nonsense attitude. I'd taken quite a few ass whoopins in my time because

The Golden Child

The depreciation of the golden child
I am not the one to hold you down.
Take a look around,
You can tell by their miserable frowns.
The nerve of these hateful clowns.
Yeah, they come with crooked smiles.
No matter how tough are the proud,
No matter what side of town.

The depreciation of the star child,
Lil one I'm here to give light
Those jeans you learned to like
Are way too tight.
Living trendy do it right.
There's many that envy
A mind that's bright.
He's your hero on the mic,
But after work he's not really the type,
Just another lie
In your misguided life.

IMITATION

Well like the average young kid, I had people I'd looked up to. The ole man, cousins, Michael Jackson. My cousins were like my older brothers being I am the oldest of my mother's kids.

Running behind those guys did a lot for my manhood. It is imperative that all young boys and girls have someone aside from mothers and fathers to be able to relate to.

I remember we lived life on the edge as young kids and that there had did something solid for me. Any child that is raised isolated or antisocial will have too much time to think and attempt to answer their own questions. Creating the possibility of them perceiving the world as being against them.

For the most part when there is inconsistency in a child's life there is also confusion. Kids have no control over the outcome of a relationship between a man and woman. When a child sees a strong mom and dad that child sees hope in themselves. There's a good chance they may perceive the world differently than a child who'd only had mom coming up. Or just dad for that matter. Either way, that sense of purpose and drive has to be instilled at an early age.

What we do to and around our kids has an effect on how they value life. I say this from experience. I have been among others that had it just as rough as I had. There was no choice but for me to become an observer of those patterns. I was once a part of those patterns. Those patterns continue to grow in our community due to a lack of values.

Children want to be a part of life. They want to be seen, heard, and spoken to. They want to be like, speak like, and look like whoever or whatever it is that is presented to them on a consistent basis. That could be mother, father, aunt, uncle, cousin, brother, sister, neighbor, famous person or anyone. They are at a stage where the mind is vulnerable and what they see hear and feel is what they will imitate.

I see the youngest little boys and girls doing things we dared not to do at their age. Not only that but it became a part of us to act with certain values without having to be reminded. For example, a girl learns to sit with her legs closed. A boy learns to stand up when he urinates. If you teach him to sit down when he urinates he's going to do just that. If there's no one to tell that precious young queen that ladies don't sit with their legs open she will be unconscious of it no matter what she wears.

Some of us do our best as to not expose our children to negative habits. Too many of us neglect the idea of being positive influences. I see mothers videotaping their toddler children doing and saying the unthinkable. Mothers who have babies while they are still in the same mind frame as their child. Age is just an indication of the amount of time you've had to experience, understand and conquer the inevitable challenges in life. If you are up in years and you have children but are still searching for attention, more than likely you're not giving enough to your child.

We fail to sacrifice our desires as adults in order to assure that our children have the necessary values to remain in self-control. It took me many miserable trips in and out of somebody's courtroom as a child and as an adult to figure out that it was my own lack of self-discipline that perpetuated my mental anguish.

Remember when I spoke of children being confused when there is inconsistency? Well look at it this way, I can remember being a big fan of Michael Jackson during his Thriller days and I will admit that as a person who appreciates creative art, I fucks with Mike! The greatest entertainer of all time, hands down! I remember I use to do his dance as if I'd created it. I'll never forget shutting down the dance floor doing the Michael Jackson. It was a Halloween party if I can remember correctly it was at a church, go figure, I was around maybe seven years old and there were kids dancing and once they'd played Mike, I'd gone into my zone. The dance floor had started to clear. There was an older kid whom I could remember challenging me. I was so caught up with everyone cheering me on and the idea of out dancing that kid, I'd forgotten that I didn't have on any socks as I did Michael Jackson's spin move followed by me stopping on the tip of my toes and raising my pant legs up revealing my ashy ankles with no socks on.

I was a big fan of Michael Jackson back then and as I started to get older more and more trends started to develop. Mike was still the man and to show you how affective the media can be on the minds of the average American viewer, I'd looked down on Mike after the whole molestation allegations, unaware at that age of how people sign up with the devil just for a shot at fame and eventually pay in the end. But I will get off into that later.

I guess once I'd hit my mid-teens, I'd lost the idea of trying to be like anyone or looking up to anyone for that matter. I would say that my going from placement to home and from here to there had started to take its toll. Well that was my inconsistency. I don't remember ever staying in one house for more than a year straight. That became a part of me, it became a learned behavior.

It had effected my trust in people. It was the result of having no discipline. Yeah I got my ass whipped when I was a kid, I'm talking ole fashioned whippings, belts, switches, broom sticks, fists you name it. One thing I can say is that I don't regret those ass whippings, they had gotten me together.

Definitely would say our future generations lack getting good ass whippings.

But even with the belts and switches, I had been missing something that no belt or any other means of punishment could replace. Good ole male solidarity. I had no sense of purpose. Lack of identity.

Never took any one serious.

I can remember the woman which whom I honor dearly to this day telling me never to back down and if I can't beat someone to pick up something and knock em in the head. That lady was my grandmother who'd passed when I was around eight or nine.

The conversations I'd had with her at five and six years old I still can recall them. This lady was realer than most men I'd met in my whole lifetime.

She'd instilled toughness that I cannot or will never lose. I will always honor her name; known by her nickname 'Pimpstick.'

Now although my grandmother was a female, she'd given me a manly value, something I could hold on to. Without a child having something to value or hope for, it's like a plant without water, the soul grows dry and bitter. I see children all the time on the internet imitating someone whom obviously influences them in a negative or positive way.

I prefer seeing kids recite black literature, or do something constructive rather than little girls doing twerk videos or saying all kinds of foul words while their parents laugh about it. I actually seen a boy no older than ten years old shooting dice with some older dudes. This kid was swearing, smoking weed you name it. I can remember being that kid. But the difference was that I'd had respect for my elders at his age. I grew up around the life and there's not too much that will surprise me. To see our kids out here doing hard drugs, disrespecting and murdering their parents is not good. Unfortunately, Nowadays you have to second guess them having guns because they are being hunted instead of protected.

I can recall being fourteen years old running around town with a sawed off shot gun I'd stolen from my ole man. I had a careless attitude. Can you imagine a child with no guidance or a care in the world running around with a sawed off shotgun under his shirt. I'd brought sixty percent of the grief I've endured in my lifetime on myself. All because I wanted to be a person who I wasn't meant to be.

So not to be religious here because I am a free spirit. And even others like me have some form of meditation or prayer if you will. Islam have the Salat, Christians have the lord's prayer or in whatever form have different prayers, Jewish has the tefillah, I can go on but the point of the matter is that those of us who believe, approach our higher powers through a communication we have different names for.

When it's time for me to communicate with my higher power instead of kneeling face down or bowing I look up. Reason being, (and this is the benefit of being a free spirit) is that why should I face down as if in shame to my higher power.

Look at it this way, when your child come to you for instruction or concern, would you want that child to have their head held low?

Wouldn't you want to see the brightness and beauty in that child's face? We were programmed to communicate with our higher power in the same manner we were forced to submit to our oppressors. On our knees begging for forgiveness and life.

The world is filled with individuals whom live their lives based on the approval of those around them.

So in other words, if there are miserable good for nothing people around an individual, then that individual will impress those people with good for nothing bullshit.

Some of us are only into impressing those that help us build and prosper. Who rely on us for leadership. Being a leader comes from studying other leaders not following followers. As long as we continue to give our energy and attention to that which compromises our peace and sense of purpose, we will never see pass what it is we submit to. We only leave ourselves vulnerable to manipulation, deceit, disappointment, and perpetuated corruptive programming.

Go to school, say your prayers, get a job, have fun, get married have kids, work hard, retire, die. Well seems to be a pretty simple way of life. But it's not that simple because while this is what society expects from you, there is no foundation of moral instruction.

Sure you have your churches, mosques, and other religious establishments but they also instill the same simple pattern through different perceptions. We're speaking of universal morale. We're not speaking of the justice system, or civil rights organizations but we need a world-wide morale enforcement targeted to prevent the crimes against all of humanity.

Our understanding of justice is based on what is presented to us unjustly. For example, if you're watching the news and before it comes on they give you a set of top stories to look forward to. One of the top stories may be that a man is arrested for shooting another man. Now in that instant without any details, we unconsciously assume that this man is the person that committed this crime. Why? Because the news said it and they're showing the guy in handcuffs being escorted by police to the back of a police car.

Which brings me to an issue that I feel the need to address. On average, a black person rather listen to the advice, information, or instruction of any other race of people (white in particular) before they will that of another black person. As if what we tell one another isn't credible enough.

We as a people have that 'you ain't my momma or daddy' syndrome. Our minds were programmed to challenge one another. To outdo each other. There were times where I was out in predominately white areas and I'd see another brotha or sista and immediately I'd get that sense of relief because there are more of my kind than just me there. But let me tell you that not all black people see things that way. There are actually brothas and sistas out here who are obviously ashamed or uncomfortable of their heritage, of their skin, of their ancestors.

Whenever a person changes their skin complexion to a lighter version you have to assume that they feel that lighter people or white people are superior and that they feel ashamed of a skin tone that is to them inferior. When did so many of our black women begin altering their body parts? Injecting poison into their souls. When did our brothas start disliking the natural hourglass shapes of our black women? For those of us who still worship our women, we haven't stopped liking it. But our sistas are given a worldly vision to envision themselves being a part of. With all the reality television shows, these women have a better chance to be on the big screen now more than ever. No matter if they have to act like clowns, expose themselves sexually, or fight and reveal personal secrets, with a good boob job and a few butt implants they can make stars out of some of these women. Black men have expectations that are so low and weak you will come to realize that these sistas are, in psychological terms, responding to a stimulus in which determines their behavior. They are simply reacting to what is perceived to them as 'no other choice' or 'gotta do what I gotta do'. Not enough strong black men to support these women. I'm speaking from a time they are infants up to the time they are grown women. I've been in relationships where I was aware of the fact that I needed growth as a man but there were times the presence of basic morals and values were questioned while I assumed that everyone automatically knows and had been surprised by the inconsideration of some of these sistas. With any understanding, you accept people for who they are with the intentions of helping that person out morally. But I'd learned the hard way that you could either lose yourself or never find yourself trying to find someone else.

THE GOLDEN CHILD (cont.)

The depreciation of our future
Young soul star
Look at what they're trying to do to ya
Planting seeds
That'll leave you weak and unfree
Instead of a leader
Wild plants can't grow
They choke throats
Introduce you to popular dope
Surround you with wretched folks
Now there you go
Putting good energy into bad hope.

The shame on our Gold
Evil lying tongues
Shaky hands grippin' guns
Lil girls just havin' fun
Reproducing bums
For a lack of discipline.

There are too many people who expect the best results from the lowest effort and attitude.

Without mistakes, correction wouldn't be necessary.

The key is having the discipline to correct yourself

Before someone else has to.

Use your mind everyone has a head.

PERCEPTION

We are born into a society that instills separation and ethnocentrism into its people.

To most of us life is about sex, money, thrills, and careless behavior. It is normal for us to want happiness. But the question is, does our happiness as individuals derive from someone else's grief? Is genuine happiness instant gratification to you as a person? Ever met someone who no matter what, always appear unhappy? You go out of your way to see them at ease but nothing seem to appease them. What makes me happy may differ from what makes the next person happy and what is grief to me may be someone else's joy. We all have different causes, reasons and interpretations to what happiness is. Happiness seems to be like opinions, and everyone has an opinion. Everyone's opinion is a result of their perception on the matter in which they are opinionating.

One Man's perception of happiness may be to provide for his family by any means necessary. Even if he has to oppress the next man's family. Genuine happiness should never derive from someone else's pain or suffering. Some people's happiness derive from seeing others happy even if it's at their expense. But my point is that thoughts are created from perceptions and in progression comes ideas and actions and from actions we have reactions or consequences.

Sometimes our perception can be deceiving and other times our perception can save us from a world of trouble. Now perception is to perceive and to perceive is to become aware or be conscious of through the senses. So I would think that we can't sense something that we have not been exposed to. Why do we as a people base our happiness on something we've never experienced? Something we never got a whiff or taste of. Because it has been instilled in our minds from birth the American dream, the piece of pie. Even when we are born into poverty we are given this illusion of paradise and happiness. And we spend our lives chasing it some of us self destruct getting too far into the illusion of this American dream. It's exactly what it is. The misconception of life. Now remember perception is what you've come to know through senses, something in which you are familiar with. How can you be familiar with just a picture that has been painted for you? We are given this illusion at young ages and those of us who are faced with poverty tends to be affected the worst by this psychological infestation of corruption. This dream has torn our communities apart. We kill and hate one another over an illusion of what will bring us paradise. No matter what your bank account is or what kind of lifestyle you live, paradise is not tangible. It can't be touched or seen. It is not perceivable. Yet we chase this paradise all throughout life and along the way we slaughter, hinder, deceive, and challenge our own people just to conclude that even with all the money and worldly power you still don't get to embrace this paradise.

We live in times when side men and side chicks are a way of life. A lot of our women have come to accept being some dudes second choice. An alternative. Even when she say that she wouldn't put up with, let her find out and she will bust windows, burn clothes, beat up rivals or what not, she unconsciously accepts it because during conversations "yo other bitch" becomes the words she uses.

The average relationship is built on the understanding of it being a 'me and you thing' and I can't remember not ever asking any of the women I'd been in commitments with the question "Do you expect me to have another women on the side?"

It's no different with us men. We complain about our women to our friends saying things like, "Man she ain't shit." Some of us like to share the most intimate details of our relationships. Then wonder how the very same ones you tell your business to literally end up doubling back all up in your business.

We lack understanding and purpose within our black households and communities. We've been reduced to experiments. People feed their families by studying the behavior of certain groups of other people who have been psychologically and economically conditioned only to use the results as a systematic way to control, divide and conquer the opportunities of those groups of people. We are simultaneously manipulated into perceiving this system as superior. In particular, those who profit from painting a picture of paradise being possible without living a righteous and peaceful life.

Those of us who choose not to determine our happiness on financial or popularity status and strive to do what is righteous and fruitful receive ridicule and disapproval from the same society that tells you to live free and aim to be financially secure by getting someone else rich.

The same society that wants you to avoid practicing morale and dignity. "Don't value pride, it will only keep you broke." They make sure to remind you of themselves once being in your shoes. Claiming to have started from nothing while all along setting you up to be in situations they would never want to see themselves in.

This book may be tossed by many, read halfway by some and understood by a few. Everyone's point of view varies according to what they've been exposed to. What they've learned to accept as making the most sense to them. The way we see things tends to wear in on our personality if not seen from an open minded perspective. You remember the expression 'being stuck in your own ways'? That's what usually derives from not being able to compromise and see things from other's perspectives. I've heard the term old fool and understand that to be an old fool one has to be continuing the same foolish mistakes as when they were younger. Because they refuse to see things differently.

I can tell you one hundred stories of how the inability to see outside of our own point of view can be affective to not only us individually but as a family, friends, business acquaintances, and so forth.

I've seen men destroyed because of their unwillingness to change their perspective on how they viewed other people and situations. They take it upon themselves to overlook the little things that matter in life. Some of us have insecure thoughts that won't allow us to consider that another brotha or sista could be going through hard times and don't want any problems but just to do what needs to be done to take care of what and whom needs to be taken care of. Some of us suffer from what others may call 'the house nigga syndrome' and with it your ability to see other people who are under the same scope and subjected to the same unjust conditions as you are as a black person, seems to be non-existent.

You will struggle with identifying yourself as black.

You will always look at your brothas and sistas as being embarrassments. It'll be "I'm not like them niggas over there." As black people we judge things the wrong way. We focus on the things that should not matter. Because we are brought up in a society that tells us we are nothing without these materialistic ambitions that should not matter. And to be somebody we hate, steal, rob, kill, lie, deceive, trick, and so many other disrespectful and disgraceful things to one another all in the name of doing better. Because we are under the perception that in order to succeed in life you must have a dog eat dog attitude.

We do things according to how we believe they should be done instead of doing what is necessary in order to survive. Perception leads to belief. Belief is practiced unconsciously making it a powerful substance.

I've learned in my recent years that a lot of the grief I'd endured, was a result of my own poor decision making. It took me too many mental ass whippings to come to the realization that there are other versions of the world aside from how I picture it. What I'd believe to be the way toward peace and prosperity only got me grief and grumpiness. There was a time when I couldn't seem to maintain my freedom. I'd be free for six months top before I ended up in somebody's youth center or jail.

Man it still burns in my mind the years I'd spent in and out of prison unable to complete a parole because I'd end up catching a new case.

Let me tell you that that was some of the most miserable living I had done. I was left with no other choice but to change my belief system. The way I had been thinking wasn't helping me. I'd acted on the wrong thoughts. Those thoughts were created by the wrong perception. I perceived myself to be someone I wasn't.

Don't be fooled by those who raise the most hell. most of the time they are cowards in hell of a situations.

BELIEF

What we believe in determines what we put our energy into. Plain and simple if you believe in Santa Claus then surely you will put your energy into experiencing the Christmas spirit. You just may put forth too much energy.

When a person believes that he/she can't cope with everyday challenges, more than likely that person will put most of his/her energy toward finding some way to escape, by way of mind altering, usually drugs or self-isolation and in some instances, suicide.

When an individual believes in something or someone so strongly, naturally energy will reproduce itself and that energy will submit to what attracts it. Under the circumstance you have opportunity. What we believe in individually forms into our actions and the lifestyle we choose to live. What we believe in as a society determines the outcome of the future.

So now I would start with our individual beliefs.

We share beliefs as we have different ones. Most of us believe in things and people whom we have never seen, touched, or heard but out of faith of what has been instilled into us we act on those beliefs. We put energy into those beliefs and over time that energy turns into spirit.

Our spirit is our essence. There are too many of our people blinded to the fact of being in control of their own peace of mind through having the necessary set of beliefs. I will not get off into what to believe in but I will say who to believe in is your own ability to use your mind over worldly matters.

A lot of the beliefs that we decide to adopt throughout our lives derives mostly from what has been instilled in us through experience, instruction, or manipulation. So for the most part we base our beliefs on experiences or as for instruction it could be someone telling you that this is what you are supposed to do or believe in doing. Now manipulation is a mixture of both experiences and instruction with the addition of misleading others through some amount trust to be frank.

This manipulation can be so tricky that the average mind is unable to realize how affective it is. Here's an example: Let's talk economics a little bit.

Now we all are somewhat familiar with supply and demand. Common sense when there is a demand for a product the prices go up and when there is not enough demand and there is too much supply the prices go down which results in all kinds of sales and clearances.

So that in itself says that we as consumers have the power to destroy or build companies.

I see so many businesses prosper with disregard for their consumers. There are businesses that profit from the ignorance of the most valuable customer. Why? Well because nine times out of ten that consumer believes that they have no better choice or can't do without whatever product or service that company provides. Everyone looks forward to when companies will put merchandise on clearance and half off sales so to clear their inventory in preparation for more up to date products. Because we believe that we can't go find another this or the services over there we can't do without we psychologically place ourselves in an inferior position which gives the company enough confidence to set us up into unprosperous contracts or stuck with products and services that produce more grief than purpose.

Our belief system can either hinder us from or pave the way to our happiness. If we believe in lies naturally as a result we will live a lie. Most of us grew up in the birth of hip hop era and as gangsta rap began to get more of a demand this ultimately was accepted as a culture and a big business for the very ones that protested it. Once they seen the potential market they embraced it and took full control of it. They made us believe that this is what we want to hear. Don't get me wrong, there are some brothas and sistas in the game who make the game what it was originally about. We all have different opinions based on our belief system of which artist is best. My best may consist of enlightment and expressing ones mind according to what the people can relate to. Whereas the next person's best may consist of trends and popularity.

I will say that we have very influential individuals set in place to create circumstance based on what they convince us to believe.

As I mentioned earlier in the book, I had been influenced by certain rappers and a few movie characters and I'm not ashamed to admit that I hadn't known any better. My belief was that what I'd seen or heard these individuals do, was how it was to be done. I had a bad misconception of reality. I based my actuality on an illusion. These individuals left the movie set and the recording studios expecting paychecks while I placed myself in those same situations and received grief and jail time. I'd nearly lost my life on a few occasions.

Ever heard of the expression 'don't believe everything you read or hear and only thing you can be most accurate on is what you see with your own two eyes'? Well that's the best advice you can hear from a person. Because of our constant 'daze' we interpret the world different from what it actually is. I found in my present mind state that I create my own stress no matter what the circumstances are. I don't base my beliefs simply on what is presented to me by others but on what is presented before me.

In other words you can tell me the what how and when but until you tell me the why I will categorize the subject at hand as manipulation which is a tactic to psychologically persuade or take control of one's subconscious thoughts through empathy or common demand. This is in itself a business. Anytime someone or something you have no understanding of but unconsciously put so much energy into, rather you want to realize it or not but you have been manipulated, tricked, jacked out of your own mental power. Our minds are so powerful but poisoned with impure thoughts and distorted beliefs. There is only one corrupted idea that successfully lasted to make a difference in the existence of mankind and that was the idea to convince millions of people that what is best for them is what coincidentally empowers not those people but the creator(s) of the idea.

The Eye 'Land

There was a man, a gun, and a snake placed on a deserted island. Nothing else existed on this island other than the natural resources of that island. The fruit trees, the gardens of vegetables, and the pure water of the surrounding body of water. There were no means of communication. No way of escaping the situation. Now this man was able to eat, drink, breath and sleep but not comfortably. There was a gun but it was just a gun. A man made tool that had no brain function. Then there was the snake. Now this snake, which was the reason that the man was unable to think, eat, drink, breath, or sleep in peace, had just as much intelligence as the man if not more. The man had the upper hand being that he was able to physically do what the snake could not.

In the man's desperate attempt to find a way other than the failed idea of using the gun to annihilate the serpent, he'd found out that not only did the gun run out of ammunition but that the bullets did nothing but cause the snake to use more intelligence in its plight to take over this land.

The man only had so much time before all of the natural resources and essentials were poisoned and rotted away. The snake was winning and the longer the man waited to come up with a way to defeat it, the more the snake reproduced and sucked the life from the island. And soon it would suck the life from the man.

The man who represents the everyday people who live for the good. The people which whom are depressed. The people that have hope. The gun which can represent a drug habit, gambling to come up on the riches that we perceive to be the solution to our struggle. The gun could be any vice or challenge we put ourselves through in order to escape discomfort or inconvenience. Then we have the snake which represents the system of evil, the greedy, the corrupt, those that profit from others misery. Those that manipulate and scheme. The island represents the mind in which the snake poisons and robs it of its natural abilities. Once the life is sucked from the island (mind) the man (People) will follow.

PART 2

PRE-CONSCIOUSNESS

CONTRADICTION

Pre-consciousness in my opinion, starts with the ability to question that which is questionable. It may sound simple but actually it is so simple that it is challenging to the average mind. Challenging because when something is accepted by everyone as the norm, questioning it will cause one ridicule and shame.

Think of the black police officers who are mentally forced to stand back and watch their white colleagues harass and violate the rights of other black people. As a black person who has at least a slight idea of the history of inequality and unjust treatment toward the black race, one has to be completely brainwashed and without a soul to be able to watch and partake in the systematic destruction of their own people.

When someone else contradicts us, we don't take it as serious as when we contradict ourselves.

Once we begin to question the things that we were taught to be as so, it humbles us in a way to where we open our minds up to absorbing more information. Now some of us are hard headed and stuck in our own beliefs. No matter who proves us wrong, we refuse to see it any other way. Some of us deny the truth because of pride, and some of us deny it because it makes us feel uncomfortable.

Contradiction can cause hate amongst those who misunderstand each other.

I was in relationships where no matter what humbling routes I took, I ended up in an argument on a daily basis. Why? Because when certain truths are exposed, you have people who cannot cope with the reality or the challenge of that truth. They will come up with any excuse or accusation to appease their shame.

I found in my life time that usually when certain individuals can't cope or understand what another individual presents or promotes, most of the time they will respond in an aggressive or disapproving manner. It's a form of defense. They will never ask you to explain yourself without sarcasm or ridicule.

Sometimes their goal is to challenge and contradict you in hopes of maintaining the false sense of security that they think they have.

A mature and secure individual is humble and wise enough to know that the truth and those who acknowledge it doesn't come in a certain look, language, or form, but is universal or diverse.

There is an issue that I want to address concerning some of the ignorance that we glorify as a people.

Now for long as I remember, I had a thirst for knowledge. I remember as a kid always into something trying to get an understanding of what was going on. I had to learn to think outside the box because there wasn't really anyone around who'd had an open enough mind to show me better ways. Once I realized that the consequences of my actions were the same old miserable consequences I immediately begin to contradict the thoughts that led up to my actions.

Sometimes as individuals we come to this realization for the wrong reasons. It's like when someone owe us money usually we don't loan them anything else until they pay us back in full in a timely manner. So we say to ourselves "I'm not letting him/her borrow another dime". But we fail to apply that same concept toward our everyday thought pattern that determine our actions and beliefs within our own will. In other words, we can cut someone else off with no problem when they've wronged us but we ignore cutting off the thoughts that lead us to nowhere. Drinking, drugging, gambling, sex, over eating, these are some of the vices we have as people and even when there is that little person on our shoulders telling us that this isn't what's best for us, we over power and bully our own subconscious into submission. We tend to accept the wrong people and the wrong things into our lives. We become blinded by infatuation. There were many of times when I'd personally felt foolish for leaning on the understanding of someone else without contradicting them.

Let me tell you all about a time I'd gone to Pennsylvania with some dudes I was hustling with.

It was around 1996, I'd just escaped from a juvenile center and decided to go on a vacation. The four to five hour drive there consisted of me being filled in on the do's and don'ts while in this small east coast town. Everyone who'd known me back in those days knew that I believed in keeping protection on me at all times. "You ain't gonna need a strap on you, they don't get down like that out here." is what was told to me. So sure enough I'd left my pistol behind and decided to play the smooth role. Now whatever you get out of this story please do not misunderstand my point.

After a few days of being there, I'd gotten my first taste of how they'd "gotten down" in this small town.

I was caught off guard while on my way to retrieve my stash.

"Come here nigga!" I heard before looking up at two masked dudes wearing all black. I immediately knew what it was. They had their pistols on me and at the time I didn't feel like running.

"Where the shit at!" They asked me before dragging me into the vacant house we'd used to stash our dope in while we sat out on the block. I can remember my seventeen year old mind racing for the right words to use to get these dudes to understand that the little dope in the stash spot wasn't worth me giving them any problems and that I've gotten down like they had. These are the words I can remember saying to this brotha who'd asked me where I was from.

"I'm from Detroit dawg! I'm just out here to get a lil money." Was my response.

"You a real nigga but this P-A." He said to me throwing me against the bath tub. I sat there looking up at this brotha while he pointed his pistol down toward my head. I will be lying if I told you that I didn't experience some type of fear but it was a fear of what was next to come. Here I was in some small quiet town four hours from my hometown where when situations like this one occurs its almost a guaranteed robbery turn homicide. I'd thought about the gun toting and stickups I'd done at my young age while that gun was pointed down at me and came to the conclusion that there was no need to beg for mercy. I guess at the time I just wanted for it to be over. But the Power that be had other plans for me. When that brotha went upside my head with that pistol, I'd played possum until they left. That experience was the result of the inability to see people for who they really were. The inability to contradict their character by comparing their words with their actions. That comparison is to match up and if it doesn't, well then you have justified contradiction.

We need to learn how to hold accountable the people who inspire us through their line of work or just their ignorance and inconsideration. That goes for corruptive rappers, crooked cops and politicians, misleading preachers, teachers, etc. And it definitely goes for the family and friends who are the roots to the soul. Black families and strong friendly bonds are broken due to the inability to accept constructive criticism and improper communication or difference in opinion.

In my present state of mind, I found that questioning that which was previously instilled in me, I'm able to move about without doubt and insecurity. My purpose becomes clearer. Learn to challenge what makes you uncomfortable, and how not to contradict your own purpose and accept what strengthens you.

WHEN THE SUN STANDS STILL

When the sun stands still
Lies are told and hope is killed
A lazy sun
When people turn fake
And stray away from real

When the sun stands still
The greedy eats the best meals
A dark sun
Means that hell is upon
When the sun stands still
Illusions and white tales
Bring out masculine women and feminine males
Promises of dark days are fulfilled

When the sun stands still
False prophets and world leaders
Make deals
When the sun stands still
Niggas are proud sleepy
And unable to feel
Damn sun won't rotate
For the future's sake
A motionless sun is
A corrupt one

CURIOSITY

When we become curious about people, places and things, naturally we search for answers in order to satisfy our desire to know.

With this being said, some of us go further than others when it comes to seeking answers. Some of us may go a little too far and beyond to find the truth. For example, a person who may be a bit curious about lions may ask someone else who have knowledge of lions and will be content with those answers. Maybe they will read some books or as they do nowadays, google lions and do some research to appease their curiosity. Whereas others may simply go where lions are and study them directly. And as always you have those whose curiosity overcomes their ability to reason and may want to risk their lives.

Curiosity is our guide to knowledge. So now it's a question of what it is that initiates curiosity within us. Individually, when we can answer this question, we will then begin to get an understanding of how much control we have over our own lives.

For the most part I can say that everything I had a passion for, rather it was good for me or not, it started from curiosity. Some things we experience by force of someone else or by circumstance but for the most part, everything we have a like or interest in, stems from curiosity. Interest is curiosity. Once we experience what it is that had us curious, we either accept or disregard it.

Personally, I have never cared for the smell or taste of cigarettes. I can remember being curious about how it was to smoke them and like most of us I tried it out. They weren't for me. They made me feel funny. I can't stand the smell of them. We've all tried out that one thing that we can never see ourselves trying out again rather its certain drugs, people, food, places, clothing, vehicles, and so forth. We all at one time or another have said to ourselves subconsciously or verbally "I'm not doing that again." Or "I'm straight on that." Either because it gave us dissatisfaction or made us uncomfortable.

Now let me explain how important associating curiosity with comfort and satisfaction is and how it affects our ability to make the right decisions when inviting people and things into our lives.

Can you remember a time when you were curious about someone or something that wasn't what they or it may have appeared ay first?

Then we say to ourselves, "I put all of my energy into that." A lot of the time, we set ourselves up for disappointment due to our own perception of value or standards I should say. We are in control of what sparks our interest. If a sista is into tall men, she will more than likely overlook ninety-five percent of the short men she encounter on a day to day basis. Now that she has told herself that she prefer tall men, unconsciously that is where her focus, interest and curiosity will be directed toward. Then she will begin to find ways to either invite or go after what she is curious and interested in.

Let's say a brotha is into dark skin women well then most likely he will focus on pursuing dark skin sistas but that's not to say that he will pass up those with lighter skin but his choice would be dark skin women. We as human beings tend to put great energy into what our preferences are because we either have an ongoing interest due to emotional attachment, gratification, commitment/pledge, or physical force which is rare in most cases.

I remember a time when Id left town with some brothas that grew up with my older cousins. These guys are quite a few years older than I am. I remember it being about ten days before my seventeenth birthday in 1995. We'd made a move out of town which had been an exciting idea during that time to me. I needed to get away and I figured I'd make a few dollars just in time for my birthday. I could remember as soon as we'd gotten off the bus, a crew of plainclothes officers had approached us and asked to search my bag. Next thing I knew, I was sitting in a juvenile jail on my birthday and sent to do some of the hardest juvenile time I'd ever done.

You see my desire to know something that was not part of my purpose exceeded my desire to be myself. Be the person that I knew I was capable of being. Yes! I'd grown up in the streets around people with all types of backgrounds and social beliefs. I'd did enough time locked up not only in my adolescent years but in my adult years also. With all of that being said, I knew in my heart that this was not the lifestyle meant for me. I'd refused to settle for or remain content with being a 'street nigga'. Even in my unconscious state of mind, there was something there telling me that I needed some discipline. Because discipline keeps curiosity from killing the cat.

When you've begun to realize that you have spent most of your life having fun fucking up, naturally you should take the rest of it more seriously.

ASSIMILATION

Let's talk about the process of taking in information or ideas. I've shared with you all a few instances where my ignorant and naïve thinking either put me in the face of danger or led me to the big house. I was more interested in perpetuating an illusion than living in a life of peace. So even in an unconscious state of mind you say to yourself, "Is this what my life is intended for?" See as long as we continue to rely on blind faith and go along with things and people which whom we don't understand, we will believe that what we are expected to do is enough for us to do. I don't want to lose anyone on that so let me explain. It's not a high expectancy for a brotha to come from the background of broken homes, life of crime, disadvantaged education, and scarcity to put together the information needed in order to realize his true purpose.

I've seen a lot of brick walls in my time and personally I could never see that as being my purpose in life. To be in and out of someone's jail for the rest of my existence on this earth. I'd had more than my share of mental ass kicking. A bright room can be darkened whereas a dark room can't get any darker it can only become brighter. So once, in our pure innocence as children we are exposed to a perpetuated illusion, our lights are turned off and we become darkened rooms of hope until some omnipresent force comes along and turn that light back on in order for us to see again.

When a child is very young, he or she will do things out of ignorance (not knowing) until that child is either frightened, hurt or discomforted by their actions. It is then the child says to themselves,

"I don't want to experience that again because it either felt uncomfortable or caused pain." This is why in my opinion, sternly disciplining children creates beautiful adult souls. When there is no one there to brighten that light by placing into that child's soul the truth, that child would be a darker version of whom they'd come from.

And even without stable parents or guidance, we process enough information to know not to do things such as place our hands on a hot stove or walk around outdoors with our bare feet in fear of burning ourselves or cutting our feet because we've probably burned ourselves or cut our feet before. So we learn to gather this information and we conclude facts through direct experience.

What about the more advanced situations in life that we've never experienced or may just be ignorant to? Of course we are all ignorant to something or some people in life. But what about those of us who grew up without anyone there to prepare us for life's expectancies. A person who is ignorant to disappointment or pain is a person who will more than likely cause or inflict it on others.

I've seen so many young foolish brothas who are sadly convinced that life is all about following trend. Copying what they've seen or heard. And this tends to affect some of us that are well off into adulthood.

If we don't have the right information to process, naturally we will process what is given to us. And this is what we distribute in return.

A computer programmer programs a computer so that it processes certain information accordingly. So let's talk about the minds of millions of children who are being programmed either in a good way or a bad way on a daily basis. Let's not forget that we have a lot of physically mature but childlike minds all around us. And just like an innocent naive child, these adults can be programmed just the same. When we are unable to process correctly the right information during our childhood the wrong information that we did gather will become our belief system and in return we program the next generation with the same distorted data. Matrix.

Imagine being born into a world where there is only one way. There is no other way known or thought about. Naturally you become part of this one way world.

And now you too knows or think but one way.

The reality of that scenario is that generation after generation is being programmed. Maybe not in a sense of learning thinking and knowing one way but the concept of using distraction in order to keep the mind vulnerable and submissive to corruptive training. A disciplined and open mind considers life and everything in it. While a follower considers just what he or she follows. If you can understand that comment, you will understand why there is so much confusion, hate, power struggle, greed, and catastrophes. Some of us, not just as a race but as human beings tend to reproduce negative ignorance by following what we were programmed to know and understand to being the most logical or easiest way.

Again when we become curious we have a desire to know about something or someone. But when you are given limited information or psyched into believing that all other information is obsolete or worthless, you are shamed of and resistant toward anything other than what you were programmed with.

The mind is a very complex function. We either use it to its fullest potential or allow it to be programmed and limited.

It is not my intention to force my opinion or lifestyle on any one but to get people to realize within themselves that as an individual there is the ability to rule their own world by reprogramming their minds through peace. In order to obtain that peace we have to look at things for what they are worth. We have to know and understand ourselves. We have to consider others' peace.

There is a paradigm that I created to understand something that was being explained in a psychology book that I'd once read. Naturally when you ask a person about it, they will say that the brain and the mind is all one in the same. Well no, the brain is an organ. Just like the heart, liver and so forth. The mind is a function of the brain. It's our conscious.

It's our reasoning or our intellect. Think of it like this; you're building a car. You have the frame, the tires and so forth. In order to driver you need the engine/transmission which acts as the brain and heart. You now have your engine and transmission but the car can't move itself. It's missing a driver. Someone to tell it what to do. It's missing its soul. Missing that which gives it direction and purpose. Just like a lot of us. We are lacking soul. We are placing the wrong drivers in our driver seats just to ride us to the junk yard. A lot of the drivers/souls we give the keys/ability to drive/ lead us to their party/misery/evil lifestyle.

We have to learn to treat bad or negative information like that food item that we will never again eat in our lives.

I am a very picky eater. As a child I use to pick my food. There were certain things I just could not put into my system. And to this day I am the same way.

I treat corruption and negativity the same. I could never rest knowing the truth and not processing it in order to distribute it so that it can benefit others who lives depend on it. Remember I spoke on consideration? In order for us to prosper individually we must enable others. It is not possible for one person to achieve greatness without the assistance of those around him. Even if it's just another driver allowing you to merge into traffic while on your way to a meeting. Please understand me here.

Some of us make life changing decisions out of wanting to fit in. We allow ourselves to be programmed into this thinking that we have free will to do as we desire. Well what if what we desire is affecting others in a negative way? Why should someone without direction or self-control have the free will to disregard those around him/her? What is more logical to me is that we were given the free will to advance what we already exist as.

Processing the wrong information can lead to self-destruction especially when a mind is vulnerable and subjected to corrupt beliefs and practices. Just think about when your child started walking and getting into stuff. Next thing you know the child was doing things that had you asking yourself "where'd the child learn that from?" Children are sensitive to information. What we give them is either detrimental or advantageous to their wellbeing.

Which brings me to a topic that I will never ignore, Corruptive Broadcasting. It's hard for a naïve mind to accept any positivity when negativity is the normal routine. As far as that naïve mind is concerned, that positive shit doesn't pay the bills.

And so this is what our young minds are carrying on into their adulthood reproducing and instilling into the future. 'Get yo money this' 'kill that'. I've witnessed so many young brothas going into the prison system with football scores as their sentences due to processing the wrong message. So many young brothas and sistas who won't get a chance to correct their processing because they are no longer with us.

I will admit that I was fortunate when it came down to getting another opportunity to make a difference in life.

Our brothas and sistas are convinced by actors and actresses that being this or that is the key to peace progress and prosperity while in all actuality this and that seems to be leading our young bright stars into dark spaces where they can no longer shine.

Information is usually a collection of facts drawn up into a conclusion. Information consists of messages that are processed according to how we perceive them.

When a mind that doesn't know any better hears the same destructive message directly or even worse subliminally, that mind will naturally embrace the message in some form or fashion.

We've all heard young kids reciting words to some popular song that they've heard over and over again. They sing along with these songs not because they understand or can relate to what is being said, but because this song has a rhythm that gets their attention, and once the rhythm becomes repetitive, the mind subconsciously embrace this rhythm and before you know it, that young mind is accepting what is being said along with this rhythm rather they understand the words or not, they repeat them.

So now let's fast forward to when they are considered adults. As adults we have those same vulnerabilities as when we were children and it is by experience that we determine what to accept or not.

Music in particular is such a powerful source of information distribution. It is through music that some of us shape whom we desire to be. See it's not so much of the concept of putting words with a beat, but just the ability to broadcast it for the ears of all humans to listen and subconsciously embrace the rhythms.

Music can be spiritually alternating and destructive to the undisciplined mind. But it's not as simple as just hearing any music. Music is cultural. Music is a collection of sounds that may have existed before mankind. I'm a big fan of music. It has gotten me through years of hard times. Some I've processed the messages wrong and others brought me temporary peace.

We all have that favorite song rather a rap song, slow song, dance, pop, country or whatever but when we hear it we unconsciously transform into an alternate state. It can be an excited state, a depressing state, or an aggressive state.

Growing up, I've heard seems like thousands of songs that I've processed and unconsciously remembered. Ever hear that song you haven't heard since you were a child but mysteriously you remember the words or rhythm to it?

Music is powerful enough to cause one to believe that they are possessed with spirits when in all actuality it's their own subconscious that has embraced the rhythm to the point of no self-control. So when we find ourselves hearing that song that causes us to have an emotional or physical reaction, we are subconsciously allowing the message or the rhythm to control our existence at that moment. Once you have a good idea of how powerful music is, you will understand the importance of marketing certain messages through it and how, rather you realize it or not, it contributes to our current poisonous state of mind as a people. Believe me, the messages we hear on our televisions and radios are not messages that sounded better than the others. It's all about air play with messages that are designed to control the out of control. In other words, if you can't perceive the message as being genuinely wrong or right for you, the rhythm will consume you and the message will misdirect you for a lack of awareness and control over your own sub consciousness. Not all music is bad. Music in itself is not bad but the messages that are put along with the rhythm is what determines its effects. Simply put if you constantly hear a song that encourages violence and chaos, than you'll more than likely, subconsciously find yourself reciting this violence.

If you hear an uplifting and gentle message often enough, you will more than likely also subconsciously find peace in that rhythmic message. A naïve mind that processes corruptive messages will store dangerous information.

WHEN I WAS WEAK

When I was weak, there were no strengthening's.
I had been a thief for robbing those wickedly.
I was a liar although the truth was somewhere in me.
When I was careless they treated me carefully.
Whenever I talked down they looked up to my stance.
I cheated and was given a second chance.
When I raised hell they praised a broken soul.
In and out of jail, I had a place to go.
But once I began to grow.
People began to act like they don't know me no mo'.

CONSTERNATION

So let's talk consternation this chapter. Consternation is when you have a sudden feeling of anxiety or stress about something new or unexpected. Throughout our lives we all experience a feeling of consternation. It's a part of growing. For anyone to tell you that they are of conscious spirit, they would have to be able to tell you a story of experiencing consternation at some point.

Imagine being fed some information and as you process this information/message you realize through logic and high probability that you've been misled or misinformed and so then with that one realization you begin to experience confusion, anxiety, sometimes stress or dismay. This is natural because for years you carry yourself confident in who you are and what you do and here come some truth out of nowhere humbling you, bringing you to realize that you don't really know too much.

Now the tricky part is rather or not you allow the consternation to humble you or do you fight the feeling and live in a one-track mind frame? Once we allow ourselves to accept humbling experiences and embrace the pain or inconvenience of it, in return we are then given the opportunity to have an open mind toward so much more knowledge and wisdom. We become magnetic toward the universe learning soul enriching things and as a result we reproduce this energy.

So imagine this concept used by those with a corrupt outlook on life. See you have people who embrace the necessary intellect in order to manipulate, mislead or hinder others. Some people will call this the traits of evil. Some people who may not believe in good or evil may say it's just the way of life. If you look at it from a non-religious but good spirited stand point, anyone who mislead or cause distress upon others for their own personal gain or for the gain of something or someone which whom they represent, you are the opposite of positive productivity and the forces of nature that reproduces this energy.

Just think about the mass murderers and the serial killers, or soldiers at war, or even some company CEOs. Think about how they at one point or another had to experience some form of consternation before they decided to become killers. The unfortunate thing about these type of people is that there's no one or nothing there to influence reasoning. If we are able to simply ask ourselves; why am I doing this? What are the possible consequences of my actions? What is it worth to me?

These are key questions I have learned to be very effective when making life changing decisions.

Let me share with you a time when I'd made a lazy decision that had cost me money and years of grief. It was around the end of 2009 I'd just turned thirty-one, two of my closest female friends had gotten murdered, I was having girl problems while in the process of being exposed to the real world in more detail than I'd perceived it for over thirty years. Talk about experiencing mixed feelings. I can never forget my mind being in a fog as I went from woman to woman trying to find something that I could never get from them.

I was into the weed game as heavy as I'd ever been during this time and I was crashing with a lady friend whom I'd always considered like a sister. I was on parole still throwing rocks at the penitentiary. There were things shown and told to me that I could not avoid pursuing further research into. I was constantly watching my back because I didn't know whom out of the people I'd embraced were waiting to put the knife in me. It was December 24, and I'd decided to hang out with a female associate for the day. I remember standing in place for a long while deciding on rather to load up with my stash for sell or just take me enough for personal use. Well in my consternated state of mind, I loaded a brown paper bag with fifteen quarter ounce sacks of weed and stuffed them into my coat pocket. See the thing about this situation is that I'd known better than to move around that wreck less but was too distorted in my reasoning.

I knew well that I wasn't probably going to sell fifteen quarter bags of weed. The sista whom I was riding with ended up not being as solid as she misled me to believing she was. But I ended up getting taken to jail where I spent up to five weeks for parole violation. The case was put aside pending further investigation. Two years later on my birthday in August of 2011, I was pulled over and name ran when it came back that I'd had a warrant. I was heartbroken because I'd known about how they will catch you up on certain charges in Flint, Michigan and will release you pending further investigation and catch you sometime down the line in hopes of possibly doing something else wrong and that's when the original charge shows up once they run your name.

But this is how it went down and I'd had a feeling when they slapped those cuffs on me that I was headed back to prison.

I was given two to six years for a two year old case in which I ended up doing four years for. So the case which happened in 2009 I was sentenced for in 2011 and came home in 2015. All because of my inability to take control of my own life.

My head was filled with smoke. I can remember those days when I walked around out of habit instead of purpose. I surrounded myself with others whom had no purpose. Once I became knowing of myself, I did not allow what I should have done to outsmart the cops to form into my thought or beliefs, but I simply held myself responsible although I'd put my trust into someone else, I blame myself for that unnecessary time I'd done caged up.

When we are experiencing consternation we are susceptible to any and all things which are poison to our wellbeing. We become vulnerable to situations and people which whom we usually have control over.

We have to learn how to allow revelation to become motivation and not consternation.

As conscious beings,
we can only move as far as our thoughts allow
us to.

FREEWILL

So when you say free will most of us perceive this as being free to live without discipline and or order due to status while some of us believe that this is simply the free will to make choices that determines our future.

Some of us believe that we have the free will to do unto others what we wouldn't want done to us. Our gift of freewill can seem like a curse when you have so much evil going on in the world.

Freewill becomes a sense of entitlement and power to the weak when granted opportunity. That young timid dude in high school can end up working sergeant in the police gang unit, your boss or worse yet the president of your country. Every day we encounter certain individuals who freely and carelessly go about their day as if no one else is as important as they perceive themselves being.

These same type of people have the freewill to open their minds in order to have a broadened view of life being more to it than just them.

There is this universal perception that has been instilled into us while we were growing up that depicts good and evil being on each side of us either encouraging us to go against our values or honor them. Is it the freewill that is being systematically erased from the equation? The freewill of our people is misunderstood for entitlement, over privileged, and disregard. When doing another human being wrong becomes a routine behavior the freewill isn't thought of as having a choice to make a right or wrong decision but the right to make whatever decision that is satisfactory to an individual desire.

Imagine a life where everyone is born acting, talking and thinking the same. Well who is there to say that any one way is the perfect way? Having freewill is like having the choice to decide between eating pork or being a vegetarian, exercising or being inactive, disciplined or impulsive. While everyone is confused with life's designed purpose, it starts with having the will to make fruitful choices on our own. What we decide to do now affects us and those around us later. Freewill coincides with the law of effect. For example; we know that if we use our bare hands to reach inside an oven to retrieve a dish it is likely to burn us.

You have the freewill to decide on wearing a cooker's glove to keep from getting burned, or wait for it to cool off.

Pain is a feeling that we've learned to associate with discomfort. Have you ever met anyone who get an adrenaline rush from experiencing pain? There are even people who are accustomed to mishaps. Don't know if I would call them type of people pessimist but I'm sure we all know someone who look forward to seeing others mishaps and misery.

Ever had that one person in your ear trying to discourage you or hinder you from hope? No matter what, they have no positive outlook on anything. These people have a tendency of being unappreciative and owning a sense of entitlement. I've encountered individuals who will jeopardize their own opportunity in order to prevent you from prospering.

We choose to keep these individuals within our universe or space.

We have so much more power over our own individual peace than we know. Having freewill is like having ownership to an island that you get to build anything you want on. With the ability to practice autonomy. We all have the freewill to become better individuals.

Some of us choose to limit our expectations and standards.

Some of us choose to push ourselves to the limit. We have people who will manipulate the poor, the unknowing, the disabled and commit people to contracts or obligations and then hit them with the 'you agreed on your own freewill'.

We all use our freewill for different purposes. Some productive some unproductive. Some of us don't understand the significance in having freewill. It is the control center to destiny.

Now you see how imperative it is that we steer our children in the right direction? Children have limited freewill. Until they reach a certain age group they are unable, according to society, to make certain decisions without the approval of a parent or guardian.

So then you wonder how come society allow our children to have say so over how their parents or guardians should discipline them. How could you give a child the option to change his or her sexual preference? With these types of practices you are taking the discipline away from that child so that when they are able to make their own decisions, they are limited in scope because they were already encouraged and brainwashed into believing that this is what the majority accepts.

It's just the same as teaching a child to hate another race of people. Sure they hear and see the adults behavior in which they will imitate. Before that child get to have an encounter with that race of people they are already bias. They don't really know why they disapprove of that race of people but all they know is that this is what's expected from them. Hatred is learned behavior not acquired through genes. It is our freewill to acquire and accept anything that prevents us from progressing.

Be free but careful in your thoughts and disciplined in your actions.

PART 3

CONSCIOUSNESS

COGNIZANCE

So we come to the section where we talk about knowing, being aware, and having the ability to perceive things in a broader scope. The ability to consider all possibilities. Common sense isn't as common as we think it should be. Your common sense may be different from my common sense but that doesn't mean that you are better than me or me better than you. There is some sense that we all have in common. That is having the sense of knowing right from wrong. Any time an individual does something to another individual and dislike or approval is expressed as a result and the same or similar act is repeated, I would assume that they are purposely and knowingly compromising someone else's peace of mind. When we know better we do better.

When we know better but decide to go against the grain, a lot of the time we end up finding ourselves miserably regretful.

Some of us feel as if whatever the consequences of our actions are, they are not too big to where it will affect our status.

Understanding energy and how the universe works in our everyday lives is important. This is something that has nothing to do with religion. This has everything to do with our own interior control.

I can recall having my parole extended because I'd refused to sacrifice having something that I felt that I needed or deserved to have. The reality was that in order to get my discharge papers, I had to play by the rules. The sister that acted as my parole officer wasn't such a bad person. She had a job to do and rather or not I felt as if she could have cut me some slack is beside the point, as long as I broke the rules I had to expect whatever came my way.

Once you wake up from a nightmare, you never want to experience the dream again. For me to do seven days in a prison setting for parole violators had awaken me from the nap I was drifting off into. In other words, I had a reality check and better believe once it came time again for me to be discharged, I had my business together.

I'd made many regretful decisions only after strongly considering the consequences or results of those decisions. These decisions has cost me grief and many important relationships that never return the same.

For the past 4-5 years I've noticed that there has been an increase in police involved shootings of unarmed black civilians. As I watch this pattern it becomes obvious to me what we are up against as black Americans. We are citizens of manipulation, trickery and deceit. Here we are in 2017 and we are reliving what our ancestors went through with being lynched and other unjustified killings of our people.

Whenever you have a police force that breaks down people's doors and come in shooting, killing young black girls and there is a question of rather it was justifiable, you're dealing with a one-sided bullying ass government. The part of the system that we rely on protecting our children, actually annihilate our children. Our children are their job security. Why? Because we fail to enlighten and prepare our young for what they're up against. Why don't we prepare them? Maybe because we are manipulated into trusting the enemy. Or maybe we just don't have the discipline to pass on to them.

I have people black, brown, and white that have called me ignorant because I state things on social media concerning the systematic oppression of my people.

I stand firm against these people. It is one thing to have the oppressors attempt to discourage or hinder you from fighting for equality and justice. But when you have your own people against you, it almost takes the fight out of you.

As I've said before, these are strategies to keep us in line. You have to give this oppressor credit for being tricky. This oppressor, this evil system in which employs and accommodates the families of the same victims they unjustly confine and slaughter.

The catch is this; they have a way of convincing these people mainly the women, the grandmothers, mothers, sisters, aunts and nieces, that the minority male is useless unless he is accepted by the mass. Let's get a little more specific here.

Since the beginning you always had your uppity slave. The 'I'm better than them niggas over there' slave. The slave that was convinced that he stood out from the others, that he/she was special. The psychology of it all is that both the massa and the slave have an understanding of whose the superior and whose the inferior. Yeah you can eat near the family, you can be the driver for the family, you can help massa get dressed and even sit on massa's lap from time to time, but by white god you better never forget who you are.

I've been there done that. As a naive black child placed in the foster system, I was subjected to this systematic way of conditioning a slave mind. It doesn't matter who we are what position we have in this country, we are products of the system. You can be an independent entity, run your own blocks, cheat taxes whatever you do at the end of the day you are supporting a system that is not designed for you to be on top. And shall you reach the top, you really won't be on the top. You will be living an illusion of paradise and riches only to realize that you are still a slave.

I am supporting the system by writing this book. Do I want to support anything that is set up for me to be oppressed? No! But I want to support the truth and the mental awakening of my people. This book is my soul. I want to sell my soul to my people because my soul is beautiful and I want it to shine a light into their windows.

Whenever there is opportunity for an individual, there is many times more the opportunity for the rulers.

The bigger the opportunity the better the slave will perform. Let me give you an example of what I am saying here.

Let's say that you want to do your community some good by being an activist and encourage economic growth and opportunity throughout your community and those communities like yours. You have to convince people to take you serious first and usually this takes money. Money! The first and one of the key elements used in mass control. But I'll come back to this.

Now after coming up with the funds to convince people that you are serious and that you are willing to pay for them to allow you access to whatever avenues you choose to take, you have to be able to fund your support. You and your support system has to be able to eat. Eating is a human need. Sleep is a human need. In the society that we live in, it costs money to do these things with comfort. Now let's talk about the marketing and promotion, the travel expenses, the paperwork and approvals. Yes everything in this world has a price even spiritual self-recognition. Everyone has to get paid so that they can pay for their priorities. Everyone is paying and getting paid, rather it's the clothing store, the liquor store, the city county building, the pharmacies and grocery stores, and so on. Every one has priorities be it they good, bad, or just plain surviving. What makes us slaves to the system is the fact that it costs to do the things that are necessary in order to live a comfortable life. Why? Because society is set up on an economical foundation that is governed by the ones that designed it. While everyone is meeting their priorities, this foundation prospers. Why? Because no matter what lifestyle you have, rather you pay taxes or you work under the table, you will still pay dues. Either you end up in an office cubicle or a prison cubicle, you will pay taxes and thus, whatever form it may come in, is what keeps a society that is based on money over morale running without ever seeing a reconstruction of that system.

Just think of when President Obama approved the stimulus checks during his first term. From big corporations to individuals, from millions to just a few hundred dollars, people got paid. Why? Well in order for the country to operate comfortably, people need to be able to honor and buy what it takes for them to live in a material society. People needed groceries, medication, gas and electric so that they can eat and groom. On the other hand, corporations needed to stay in business so that they can make profit off the people that received the few hundred dollars. So it was like taking their own money and investing it back into the foundation. A way of encouraging a form of patriotism. How? Because if you received a check you either spent it right back in someone's business where you paid taxes, which went into their accounts where they would pay taxes. If you ended up saving it in a bank, it has been used to generate interest which has a tax on it that goes to the foundation. And if you spent it on drugs or somewhere where you didn't pay taxes, then you probably had to go buy something from a store that you needed in order to use the drug. And the dealer eventually pays by spending his money on something where he had to pay a tax or worst catches a case and now he/she becomes a new account for the foundation. So see how it works? Everything the people of the foundation does returns money that generates revenue back into the foundation causing the foundation to operate, grow, and rule.

Very necessary when your foundation hits a downturn known as a recession. When there is a recession there is a question of dependability amongst the people of the foundation and so there comes challenge of superiority in which the foundations power structure becomes at stake because you no longer can convince people of your vision.

This is why certain truths are not revealed voluntarily. One has to have the open mind and courage to be able to want and grasp the truth. Finding out the truth and redefining who we are as individuals is like detoxing out every impurity within your mind and body and feeling the difference.

I can remember being attacked by some white dudes in prison. It was an incident that changed a lot about me.

It had pushed my tolerance for unnecessary behavior over the edge. That applied to others disregard for my space and including my own behavior.

I'll always remember watching a Michigan versus Michigan State basketball game. I had a bet placed on the game that I was watching on my cellmates TV. I was so caught up into the game that I'd uncharacteristically allowed myself to be snuck from behind. The blows to the chest startled me but it was the object that had been used that concerned me. My adrenaline mixed with confusion exceeded any pain

I may have felt at the time. Once it had registered that someone had stuck me, I wanted to know who over the why because I'd felt violated and pissed off that I'd allowed someone to catch me slipping. I'd made eye contact with the white boy before charging at him. I'd blinked out. At that time I did not consider any size or toughness he may have had over me. I did consider that he was swinging a homemade pick at me in which he had already stuck me quite a few times with. I decided to accept whatever fate that awaited me.

I was sure if I could connect a few punches that I would either knock him out or make him drop the pick.

I was willing to take a few more stabs preferably to the arms but during that time I just wanted revenge.

That's when I found myself fighting two white guys now instead of one. Before long there was another one and while I was getting punched and stuck, I felt no pain just adrenalins that began to fade away. It was only when I noticed the drops of blood that fell to the floor did I feel my energy dying away. It was then they decided to back off.

I'd realized that I needed medical attention. I could not stand the fact that I was too weak to kill all three of them and it was a tough pill to swallow.

Eventually they'd met their fate, within an hour they were being attacked by a prison unit full of angry brothas of various faiths and social organizations. When I saw them walk past me in handcuffs battered and bruised, I felt just a small piece of relief but it wasn't enough.

This was one time in my life that when it felt good to see our people stand up for a cause. To this day I could not tell you a more logical reason as to why I was set up to be stabbed which ended up being more of a 3on1 fight instead. Maybe a year later I ended up seeing one of the guys in another prison. For over ten months, I walked past this dude with all the discipline I had. It had crossed my mind many times to put together a way that I could take him out without being caught. At this time I had already been denied parole and was going on my fourth year and had only been sentenced to two. I was due to see the parole board and I tell you no lie, I wanted to be free.

I've had conversations with guys who'd turned a few years into life sentences because they felt it was worth it at the time. Every day of every year I'd spent behind them walls, I told myself that if I could make it to be free that I would do what I needed to do to avoid any bullshit that would jeopardize that freedom.

I found myself into more fights and conflict than any other trip to the Michigan Department of Corrections. I was in the midst of a mental breakdown. There was a side of me that said accept the fact that it may be my destiny to be in and out of prison and that I needed to be more aggressive than mindful. And then there was the side of me that studied, read books, wanted peace, loved to learn and do right by others. I gambled, I hustled, fought because I thought it was necessary in order to survive. What I knew was important toward gaining the peace was having the ability to think with logic and patience for the repairing of my broken soul. These are qualities that makes a beautiful person. I've always admired being beautiful.

Naturally, I have flashbacks of that day. And it is an incident that will always be used to remind myself of how strong and disciplined enough I am to face and overcome any challenge that may come my way.

We all have the choice to make decisions but we do not have the choice to decide the consequences of our actions.

My manhood isn't determined on trend or what others believe or think I should believe or follow.

ELIMINATION

So when we say elimination we are referring to the complete removal or destruction of something or someone. When we as people learn to use this elimination before we experience inconvenience or mishap, we will see the importance in sacrifice. I like to relate the words elimination and sacrifice due to the fact that when we as individuals decide to let go of people, situations, and things that doesn't coincide with what makes us greater individuals, we eliminate as in get rid of or make a sacrifice which also has a non-religious meaning of being the act of giving up something valued for the sake of something else regarded as more important or worthy. So we make sacrifices by eliminating. Elimination and sacrifice is human nature. But we tend to use this process toward immediate gratification oppose to solidifying and securing our greater selves.

I've definitely had to make sacrifices by eliminating those people and things that brought out the worst in me. To understand power and control, rather its over our own selves, we must know sacrifice and elimination. There comes a time when challenging decisions need to be made where we have to use reason over emotion. Think about when you have a limb or other body part that is infected and you are given a choice to either keep that part that can spread toward your other body parts and limbs which can result in fatality or make a sacrifice by eliminating that part and saving the rest of your existence from infection. Seems to be an easy decision to make but not everyone is mentally able to use reason over emotion or unreasonable attachment.

We tend to love and bend over backwards for others who won't do the same for us or who uses us and act two-faced which is poisonous acts to the soul. They are like cancerous limbs that have to be eliminated. By making that sacrifice we save our souls from further bitterness and unwanted grief.

We have to learn to control emotions such as love and lust and use reason. Most of us put ourselves in dangerous and unhealthy situations due to having the inability to eliminate and sacrifice destructive people and things.

When you use elimination and sacrifice as a tool to gain power over your own being, you pretty much are able to create your own circumstances. Some of us are reluctant and refuse to give up certain things that brings us joy or pleasure even when we know the consequences.

Every one of us have a story to tell about someone we know that met their demise by refusing to make the sacrifice necessary by eliminating that which was unproductive or caused them pain, suffering or inconvenience. Women that held on to abusive men, men who'd trusted wicked women, brothas and sistas who'd refused to give up the street life or addictions. The list goes on.

In an inspirational audio I study said that grown people have no patience for negativity. And this is an area I continue to work on as far as my reaction to ignorance.

I'm peaceful but far from flawless. It bothers me to see people so miserable that they proudly boast about it and refuse to acknowledge when they are wrong let alone correct their inconsiderate actions. And this is why we have so many young deceased brothas and sistas. This is why our elders are not being respected and for the most part has given up black hope.

This is why most of our hope is in the system giving us an individual chance one lucky day. This is why we have the national lottery, dreams of big nice houses where "great American neighbors" don't want us in their communities, nice cars, my organization is holier than yours establishments, and where the focus is on maintaining a status oppose to welcoming lost souls and instilling hope into their hearts and minds.

I can go on. So many distractions. Not enough enlightening.

It's next to impossible to wake up a tired drunk compared to a casual drinker.

Sure we all have our own way of living and for the most part we all live for the convenience of our own. Refusing to sacrifice the good tasting unhealthy food in order to purify our bodies prevents us from eliminating health problems that we pass on through our genes to our offspring. Refusing to sacrifice unproductive and poisonous family members, friends, mates, jobs and such in order to move on and replace with more productive genuine people and opportunities prevents us from eliminating failure, stress, missed opportunities in life, growth, peace and happiness and anything else that is joyful and prosperous.

We are to stay loyal and committed toward our family but only if our individual families are loyal and committed to us. Love can be blind sometimes. There are savage individuals who prey on their own love ones and they eventually devour them based on an assumption of love.

There comes a time when we as individuals have to make sacrifices by eliminating that which is useless toward our being. Sacrificing by eliminating isn't easy at all. Especially when it comes to drug habits, love, money, lust, pride and so many other powerless excuses. I have to have this drug or I have to have her/him and I need that money to get this or that. We psychologically trick our minds to make inessentials necessary in our unknowing lives.

Know how to use people and things according to their value in order to gain and maintain control over what is produced through dealing with them.

A solid thought is more powerful than five weak friends.

MODESTY

When we are able to eliminate poisonous people and things we are able to accept modesty more proudly. We find peace and comfort in who and what we become. Being around demons and embracing mishaps tends to cause us to match the unnecessary energy and instill bitterness to where everyone believes that they have to be hard in order to survive. In my experience I've found that the average person walks around throughout the day wearing a mask of the same person who causes them grief and mishaps. The person who hinders them from learning any better. Who convinces them that what they know is all there is to knowing about life. Feeding their minds whatever poison that prevents it from being open to the concept of action and reaction, consequences, creation of circumstance and the sort.

This mask prevents modesty: the absence of self-assertion or sense of entitlement, arrogance, and presumption. Being modest is respecting one's own merits. Being modest is being humble. Being modest is knowing how unnecessary hardships arise from foolish and arrogant tenancies.

We try too hard to be the wrong people. Peace produces self-security. It promotes confidence in who a person is. A lot of the time it takes mental ass whippings for some of us to become humble. Sadly to say, some of us are humbled through physical mishaps. With physical discipline doesn't always come the essential elements that produce the right understanding of self and of life. Being modest is considered weakness amongst ignorance. The same ignorance that usually becomes modest as a result from being ignorant.

I can share with you all how modest I continue to become as I write this book. During the time it took to create this book, I experienced some of the most challenging situations in my lifetime. And they were some tough and humbling challenges. At times I wanted to give up on this book.

But then I remembered that I had hyped it up and put so much hope into it that the person whom I've became as a result of a life of adventurous mishaps, was depending on me and that it wasn't about me. It isn't about who pisses me off or who I can't reach out to. It's about the purpose and the purpose consists of the wellbeing of those of hope and prosperity through self-awareness and peace. It is intended to reach those who are like I was at one point and never again want to become.

I made a pledge to my righteous self that I will never again willingly allow poison to consume my reasoning.

It seems almost impossible for a man that grew up amongst arrogant savages and has history of being an arrogant savage to retreat toward self-awareness and return to an arrogant savage atmosphere without resorting to his own arrogance and savageness as a means to survive.

It's like a heroin addict kicking the monkey away only to go to where he use to buy the heroin at in an attempt to convince all the other addicts that there is a better way while being offered the joy of the dope everywhere he turns.

Yes it feels good to tell people about themselves when their demons are invading your space, but when we put ourselves on the same level as them, those demons become us and before you know it we resort to the ways of the weak as a way of trying to communicate with them.

I've found that a lot of miserable people suffer from a lack of sense of purpose. They believe that their joy and success comes from the misery of others so they tend to cause misery upon others in order to replace their own misery with this illusion of joy.

Imagine the modesty it took for our great leaders to have had in order to take the pressure of systematic racism and the negative criticism from some of the very same people who they fought for and was able to leave an impact on generations to come.

Brothas and sistas like Malcom X, Marcus Garvey, Assata Shakur, Harriett Tubman, just to name a few. These are individuals who decided to take a stand against the unjust conditions that were put upon them and their people.

When we don't stand for something we will fall for anything and as a people we fall more and more for the same garbage that keep our minds closed.

Modesty is mocked by those who have the perception that life is about aggression. Only the strong survive. Dog eat dog.

This is the mind-set that we learn to acquire throughout some of our lives. Everyone is so determined to outdo the next. It's like we live in a mental jungle. Where survival is natural and greed is necessary.

That's just how important it is for an individual to know themselves and what his or her purpose because when you establish peace within, what others value you as is internal.

A modest person is a confident person. Confident in the way they move, which is careful. You cannot cause shame on a modest person because modest people tend not to partake in actions that will lead to shame or embarrassment. When we know better we do better!

What sense does it make to prove to another human being what kind of person you are or what your intentions are if they are unable to observe good intent through your actions? If you find yourself having to explain what's good, then maybe it is best that you evaluate your intentions because good intent is obvious to the good eye.

When people question your good intent, it's not always that they don't know your positivity, sometimes it is because they are intimidated by it.

I've learned over the years that hateful people refuse to acknowledge the good in those that they are intimidated by. Some demons will go the furthest extent in order to block out your positivity. Why? Well because for the most part goodness doesn't coincide with the emotional and spiritual structure of a wretched person. It's like mixing oil and water.

Ever go out of your way to try to cheer someone up and whatever you do or say they counter your good vibe negatively?

I've witnessed people humble themselves even when they knew that they weren't in the wrong, all for the sake of peace only to be accused of being the devil by the devil.

Some people will steer you toward the same messy table they like to eat at if you don't stand firm and let it be known that you prefer eating amongst cleanliness.

Having a bitter heart can be worse than having a heroin habit. You can escape your misery through temporary pleasure only to come down from the high and realize that you're in worse shape than the last rush and that the bitterness never vanished.

THE NOTICE OF INTENT

When I noticed that I was weak
It did not sit well with me
So I embraced toughness
And became stronger

When something scared me
I was ashamed of being a coward
So I challenged it
Became fearless

When I was tired of being foolish
I began to think before I moved
And wizened my foolish self-up.

ACTUALIZATION

Who are you? Where do you come from? Why are you here?

What is your purpose? When we can answer these questions as individuals on a regular basis, we could grow out of the daze and into reality. The reality is that as long as we live by obstruction oppose to good instruction, we will continue to be susceptible to manipulation and misinformation.

We will remain like chess pieces in a game being played by our own manipulated mind state versus a systematic oppressor. Imagine being controlled by your own demons and a biased system that stack the cards against you. Unless you are open minded this concept will confuse you.

Have you really thought of your purpose? Or are you just here to die? If you are just here to die then you probably have already died spiritually. If you are here breathing in good air but in return you give the universe hell, you are part of the force that creates hopelessness amongst generations of potentially great leaders.

If your purpose is for your own wellbeing you are not doing the world any good. This is why we have ghettos because mentally there is inconsideration and greed throughout our communities. For the most part, we lack brotherhood. We lack unity.

Black people should not have to be a part of anything unproductive just to have a sense of protection and or acceptance. Why become a part of anything that coincides with the same thing the oppressor has in his book of chess strategies?

This literature is not just intended for black people but a suggestion for all colors and nationalities that are oppressed rather by a corrupt unjust system or by their own misperception of what their purpose in life is.

At the end of the day we live our own lives. But without purpose we pretty much are puppets being controlled subliminally by our own foolish will. In other words, we are given ultimatums of the lifestyles that either, lead us toward peace and determination or misery and contentment. What becomes of our souls is the result of either being humbled by our own humiliation or arrogant in our own foolishness.

Wise is the soul that lives according to the paths direction. When you walk into a flower shop, your intention would be to buy flowers or learn about something that has to do with flowers oppose to if you were to just wander into a flower shop inquiring about auto parts. You are either up to no good, blind, or have some sort of mental impairment if you were to do that.

So let's use the same concept with life. For the most part, when you decide to mind your business and that which affects you, stay away from that which does you no good you're to the point where you are comfortable and secure in who you are. You have learned that in your experience that this way is the most productive and convenient way for you.

We only bother ourselves with situations that are not meant for us if we are up to no good. (Being nosy, trying to get down on someone, hating, etc.) Blind which could represent being unconscious or unwilling to be aware. And then the mental impairment could represent the inability to know what one is doing. Either way we tend to learn and have an understanding of our specific purpose which we are comfortable with accepting by following natural living.

We all have heard such sayings as "never go against the grain", let nature take its course", and "if it isn't broke don't fix it".

These are all ideal expressions of wise living according to the direction of your path. Simply put, if your path seems to be leading you nowhere or is causing you perpetuated mishaps and grief, it may be wise to change paths which could mean changing your thought pattern.

If the path you are on appears smooth with little to no potholes or obstacles, then stay on that path even though it seems like you'll never stumble upon treasure just ride it all the way out because eventually you'll produce greatness by dropping seeds of value that'll grow just like you did on that path making it legendary.

To come to the realization of the power that we have over our own lives, we have to stop taking our existence for granted. We have to put as much attention and energy into the inner person as we do our exterior selves.

For instance, I'm a guy that likes to take pride in my appearance. I know the time and effort it takes to groom and get my attire together. As people we don't put much thought into that. We over look these small things because they become so routine throughout the course of our lives that they are no big deal. But anytime we put the smallest of energy into something that is routine, subconsciously the energy is trained to apply itself.

So being this person who takes pride in his outer appearance, it will be confusing to not have the ability to apply the same energy into primping my personality, my inner being, my soul. This is challenging.

I was given something to think about by someone who hadn't seen or heard from me in over ten years. They told me that I talked too much. I didn't take offense to it but I took heed to it. I embraced and reconsidered my approach when it comes down to motivating others. Others who have no ear for motivation. Now this person wasn't particularly in a position to give me any values but from the mere fact that she hadn't seen me in years and was able to point out such thing without any hard feelings behind it, I had to consider what she was saying as a strength and not an insult.

When it comes down to life, we have to understand that most people and situations we encounter exists according to our own decisions. Sometimes we have no control over who or what we encounter and usually during those times we are children and are subjected to whatever the results are of the adult's decisions.

I think as competent adults we have become careless by this American society's way of living when it comes down to morals and values. Ever wondered what it will be like to live in a world where we all treated one another equally and without bias? No matter where you go, everyone seems to be in competition in some shape form or fashion.

Power is the ultimate goal. Rather its power over the world or one's own household, we all go out of our way to get the money that we believe it takes to bring us the respect that gives us the false sense of power.

You will have people either misunderstand or simply try to discourage you from having a productive purpose. They will try to convince you that you are wasting your time and that no one cares. The truth of the matter is that these people will not try to convince you that they themselves in particular do not care and it is probably them who you are wasting your time on.

With so much negative energy flowing throughout the lands of the earth, it seems almost impossible for the world to exist another one hundred years. There's too much of a power struggle in which everyone uses a self-righteous reason as to why they are struggling over this imaginary power.

Think about those individuals who are spending the rest of their lives in solitude because they felt that they had power over someone else's life. We are not speaking of those individuals who were put in a situation where they had to protect themselves or their families, but the ones who felt violated to a point where the only power between them and the other person was the gun that they'd had the advantage of having in their grasp.

Now no matter how you look at it, the only true power we all possess comes from our ability to use discipline, logic and purpose. Whenever we lack the mind to reason with ourselves, it doesn't matter how big of a gun, crew, gang, organization, army, or followers we may have, it is limited.

Limited to emotional discrepancy which is not just toward those who stand behind us.

We tend to take advantage of people's dedication toward us by involving them in our bullshit. This is a way of abusing what we consider power. Ability is power. The more advanced the ability is, the more significant is the power. Yes we can pull the trigger to a gun to take someone's life or even call a few shots but the real power comes from the ability to out think the weak and wicked. To create greatness through truth. When you can leave an everlasting effect on people's thoughts, you are powerful. Just like the truth is powerful, a lie can be just as powerful but not for as long. A simple lie can have an effect on generation after generation of people before it is out powered by the truth.

A simple verse to a song can have so much of an impact on a people's lifestyle that it becomes repeated. A lie can turn into a power supply for the weak mind. Money can't be the root to evil, it's the wrong purpose and understanding of what true power is.

We have power over our children while our bosses, pastors, welfare agents, police, and whomever else we may report to for whatever reason have power over us. Some of us become depressed in this cycle of power structure. Why do you think that that may be the case? Well because there is no control over one's own mind. Yes others may have power over you when you are unable to suppress your unhealthy thoughts and control your actions.

When we are in control of our own thoughts and actions in a logical sense, no matter whom it is we may report to, we have the power to create our own circumstances and are not reliable on someone else's program that which doesn't coincide with our own or does us any good.

When you value yourself and know how much you are worth,
  You refuse to play as someone's underling.

Don't share your spiritual diet with everyone, some people can't stomach what you bring to the table. No need for a wasted good meal.

AUTONOMY

Autonomy is self-governing. Once you know in your being that you have what it takes to recondition your life, you will become autonomous in your mind and so will you in your actions which in return according to the rules of gravity, you will receive back what you put out. Remember the expression what goes around comes around? It's a scientific fact. Once we realize this, our actions become calculated out of wisdom. Experience causes us to either accept or avoid people or situations and if there ever come a point where we're in between then we are slaves to random circumstances. We will continue to repeat the history of our individual lives. Make the same mistakes, put up with the same people that can't contribute to our peace of mind and wellbeing but adds to the stress that we endure.

I'd spent more than enough of my thirty-nine years in and out of people's institutions until I came to the realization that until I started thinking for my present and future and not for my past, the past will always be my reality. There are individuals whom we see out here in the world on a day to day basis that are mentally and spiritually incarcerated. It reminds me of the old saying, "You ain't gotta be in jail to be doing time." Think about that!

Ever see people walking around so mad that it becomes who they are identified as. Their frowns becomes permanent scowls on their faces. I use to be a frowner. It didn't work out well for me because I rather smile. I'd endured so many mishaps in my lifetime that I was forced to take it with a glass of water. I couldn't use 'life isn't fair' as an excuse to continue to frown.

Sometimes when I wanted to be bent out of shape for some reason or another some force within me would make light of the situation and all I could end up doing is shrugging my shoulders and smiling at the adventurous life I live.

I can remember an experience that will always be embedded in my memory. After this particular experience, I was able to place myself in the slavery and Jim Crow era. It was around August 2004 maybe a week or so after my twenty-sixth birthday.

I can recall going back and forth from Detroit to Flint on a public bus route which required traveling through several other small towns. One of the towns being Auburn Hills, Michigan where the Detroit Pistons had played since the early 90s up until 2017.

I was on a late night run to meet with some young white guy I'd just met to sell weed to. It was around 1 a.m. and being in a rural area I will not front and say that I wasn't cautious of the wild animals lurking or skunks and raccoons. Almost at my destination, I felt the need to check behind me when I noticed two aggressive walking white dudes. There was no need to ask questions or compromise, I was out in the boondocks by myself at 1 am in the morning, no pistol or any other protection. This scene had reminded me of too many Jim Crow era stories I'd read. Usually I would have challenged them but under the circumstances, I didn't know what they were working with as I wasn't working with nothing but arms and legs in which I put to use.

There was a gas station just ahead and I remember running toward it and as I neared it coming from the other side of the street, I was met by a SUV truck. I will never forget looking into the face of the young white girl who drove it barely running me down before I made it into the parking lot of the gas station. My intention was to be where there were lights and eyes. I was naturally prepared to square up with those boys. But I damn sure wasn't about to allow them to gang up on me where they can get the best of me and abandon my body somewhere. I ran straight into the store without noticing the clerk out in the lot watching me being chased by five angry looking white people. I'd found out later that he'd called the police as I'd expected although I didn't see him while entering the store. I stood in the back of the store's cooler area ready to protect myself on camera and where there were lights. Now as I stood there obviously waiting on the white mob to come in or either the police, I felt somewhat relief because as we are brainwashed into believing that the police is there for the protection and safety of the public. But unfortunately for me this wasn't the case on this night. I stood there adrenaline running wondering what in the hell was wrong with these people. Were they on some late night lynching nonsense? Were they drunk and hated blacks? Before I knew it, I seen the man in blue with his gun drawn on me telling me to put my hands up. "What's up I'm the victim!" I remember telling him feeling my temper rise. I tried to calm down thinking that maybe they're just taking precaution. But then after I'd ask the officer why were they placing make in handcuffs, he stated that the mob were claiming that I tried to steal two of their vehicles and tried to break into their home.

It was not the first racial discriminating encounter I'd had and it definitely wasn't the last. I can't tell you all of the emotions that ran through me as I was placed into the back of that police car. I'd explained to the cop that all I was doing was walking to meet someone and to catch the bus that takes me to Flint.

It was so simple for a house of five white roommates to see a black guy walking down the street at 1am in the morning and decide to chase him for whatever reason, and after he runs into a gas station and the police shows up, they tell the police lies that there is no evidence to support. Of course I'd taken it to trial. I was on parole for drug dealing while stealing cars and home invasions weren't my M. O. I had only been out for 7 months prior to that happening. Now here I was sitting in the Oakland county jail where I'd begin to develop a deep resentment toward the justice system and toward racist and arrogant whites.

I did a hard four months going to trial. Fights, insubordination toward the guards, cursing people out. The stomach ulcers that have bothered me since my teens had been giving me problems and it didn't help that I did not eat pork meat or am a picky eater because the food they had served was slop. I'd lost weight and was stressed out. Developed temporary alopecia.

At the end of the day it was their word against mine and although there was no evidence showing that I tried to steal their cars or break into their house, the judge who was a crooked one had pretty much coerced the all-white jury into finding me guilty with faulty jury instructions. They'd laughed about how quick it took to find me guilty after the jury findings. I was found guilty of attempting to steal a car and attempting to steal out of the car. Just because a group of white roommates said that I did.

The whole court procedure was a railroad. The arresting officer was also involved at the infamous Palace brawl where the Detroit Pistons players and fans fought it out with the Indiana Pacers players and he'd used it as an excuse of being tired during his testimony. When it was all over I was sentenced to two 1-5 year prison terms as a habitual offender and I ended up serving over two and half years. For being a black man already on parole. I was the only black face in that courtroom during my trial. Everything around me that day was white except the robe that the judge had worn. That experience had to be the worst when it came down to dealing with blatant racism.

It was experiences like this that molded me into the strong minded person that I am. After living hard for so long I've learned to appreciate the opportunities to live a easier life. I'd put too much of the wrong energy into accomplishing more than enough of the wrong things in too little time at too young of an age. Moving too fast will usually cause us to run into something that either slows us down or kills us.

I had to learn how to govern my own thinking process. There is no way male or female can you call yourself fully grown if someone has to instruct you on doing what it is you already know you should be doing.

We lack autonomy as a people. We rely too much on the oppressor to inform us of what's best for us. Think about what you just read. Yes! Anytime you hear black people say that it's Gods doing when hurricanes destroy the lives of so many blacks and other minorities. How can you say its Gods doing when police are shooting down brothas and sistas like it's a sport?

To me, that's just like saying that God doesn't like minorities.

But still this is not a religious issue, I brought that up to identify the importance of governing our own thoughts and actions. We have to understand that until we do learn how to govern our own thoughts we will continue to be manipulated and lied to.

We will perpetuate focusing on status instead of character.

Consideration promotes peace.

Desperation has a tendency of trying anything, even if it's detrimental to its own existence.

To know life you have to have control over you own.

LIVE IN PEACE!

ACKNOWLEDGEMENTS

I would like to thank everyone who influenced me with the energy to create this book rather it was good influence or negative vibes I thank you!

ABOUT THE AUTHOR

Rio Delores born in Detroit, Michigan to a young teen mother is the eldest of ten kids.

Growing up he'd experienced worse than what the average child experiences during their childhood. At the young age of eleven, he became familiar with the courts and it wasn't long before he was a ward of the state. He'd made his way throughout the juvenile halls, boy's centers and foster homes of Michigan.

Ultimately, his behavior led him from the juvenile halls and into the adult jails.

Rio Delores having an epiphany, decided to utilize the intelligence, education, and experiences to encourage and inspire others. He has written several unpublished novels based on his rough experiences in the streets.

He has a concentration in business management, owns Rio Delores Services based in Scottsdale, Arizona where he resides. Rio Delores who also writes under the name Amiti Xolani writes poetry and is involved in humanitarian work. You can visit his website at www.riodelores.com for inquiries.

Printed in the United States
By Bookmasters